CYBER THREATS

PHISHING

FOCUS READERS NAVIGATOR

by Connor Stratton

WWW.FOCUSREADERS.COM

Focus Readers is distributed by North Star Editions:
sales@northstareditions.com | 888-417-0195

Produced for Focus Readers by Red Line Editorial.

Photographs ©: iStockphoto, cover, 1; Shutterstock Images, 4–5, 8–9, 11, 14–15, 17, 18, 20–21, 22, 24, 26, 29; Mindaugas Kulbis/AP Images, 7; Red Line Editorial, 13

Library of Congress Cataloging-in-Publication Data
Library of Congress Cataloging-in-Publication Data is available on the Library of Congress website.

ISBN
979-8-88998-519-8 (hardcover)
979-8-88998-580-8 (ebook pdf)
979-8-88998-551-8 (hosted ebook)

Printed in the United States of America
Mankato, MN
082025

ABOUT THE AUTHOR

Connor Stratton writes and edits nonfiction children's books. He lives in Minnesota.

TABLE OF CONTENTS

Google

CHAPTER 1

A $100 MILLION PHISH

In 2013, Google's **accounting** department received an email. The email seemed to come from a tech company called Quanta Computer. In the email, Quanta asked to be paid for work they had done. Bills and other documents were attached to the email.

In 2013, nearly 50,000 people worked for Google.

Quanta often did business with Google. So, Google's accountants made the payments. They sent money to a bank account. They believed it was Quanta's account. By 2015, Google had paid $23 million to the account.

However, Google had fallen for a phishing attack. A man in Lithuania set up the crime. He had worked with others to trick Google. The Quanta email had come from a fake address. The **financial** documents were fake. And the bank accounts were not Quanta's.

Meanwhile, the phishing group pulled the same trick on Facebook. Facebook ended up sending $98 million. Two of

Law enforcement caught the Lithuanian phisher in 2017.

the world's largest companies had been robbed of millions.

Law enforcement got involved. In 2019, the phisher was sentenced to five years in prison. Google and Facebook got most of their money back. Even so, the crime showed how costly phishing could be.

CHAPTER 2

HOW IT WORKS

Phishing is the act of sending a message that seems real but comes from a fake source. Phishers want to gain something. They typically seek personal details, passwords, or money. Phishers often pretend to be banks or credit card companies. They use email, phone calls, text messages, or social media.

Phishing is the most common type of cyberattack.

The word *phishing* sounds like *fishing*. That's because the actions are similar. A fisher uses bait to attract fish. Then a fish gets caught on a hook. In phishing, the "bait" is the message. A victim who receives the message is the "fish." The victim gets tricked into doing something. In that way, they get caught on a "hook."

Phishing takes advantage of how people tend to behave. For example, people are likely to follow directions from their bank. So, a phisher may pretend to be a victim's bank. The phisher says the victim's account will close. To stop that, the victim must confirm their account details. The victim gets tricked.

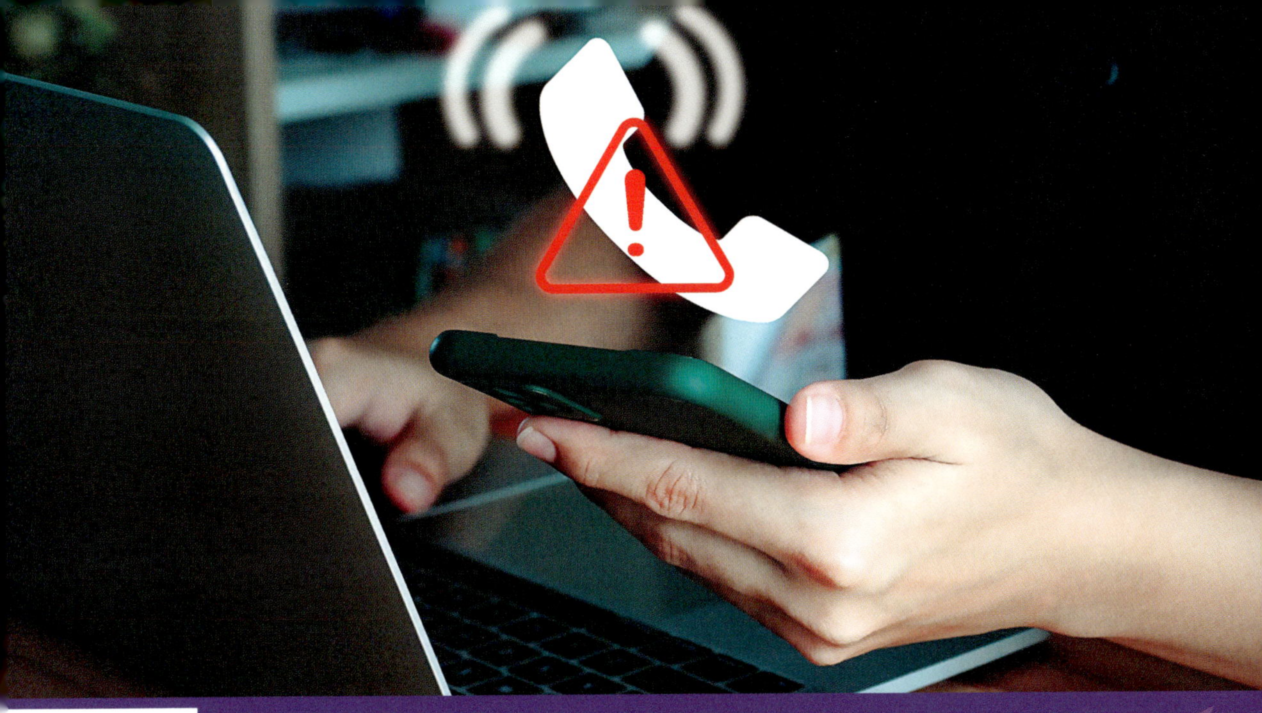

Phishing messages often use words such as *important* to catch people's attention.

Phishing messages often include links. The links go to fake websites. These sites look similar to real ones. People may not notice. So, they input their details. Phishing links may also contain **malware**. That allows phishers to **hack** computers.

Sometimes phishers send general messages to thousands of people. The trick may work on only a few victims. But that can be enough for phishers to make money. Other attacks are called spear phishing. That is when messages target specific people. Spear phishers study their targets beforehand. For example, they may learn the name of a person's

AI PHONE PHISHING

Some phishers use **artificial intelligence** (AI). This technology can create fake voices that sound like real people. Sometimes people receive phone calls from phishers. The voices sound like loved ones. They say they are in trouble and need money right away. Some victims get tricked. They send the money. The phishers keep it.

boss. Then they send messages using the boss's name. These details make the messages seem more real.

PARTS OF A PHISHING MESSAGE

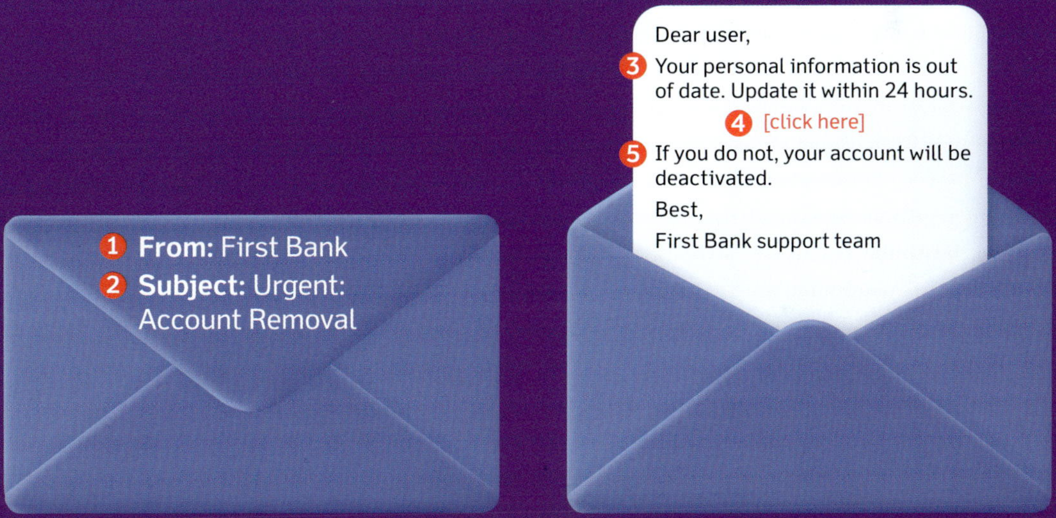

1 **From:** First Bank
2 **Subject:** Urgent: Account Removal

Dear user,
3 Your personal information is out of date. Update it within 24 hours.
4 [click here]
5 If you do not, your account will be deactivated.
Best,
First Bank support team

1. **Official-sounding source or sender**
2. **Subject that grabs attention**
3. **Request for information**
4. **Unsafe link**
5. **Threats of bad consequences**

CHAPTER 3

PURPOSE AND IMPACT

People use phishing for many purposes. One common goal is identity theft. This is when the phisher pretends to be another person. The phisher starts by stealing the victim's personal information. Then, they use the victim's bank account or credit card. They spend lots of money.

A person's phone often contains a lot of their personal information.

Other phishers send messages with ransomware. Ransomware is a type of malware. It locks the victim's device. The phisher holds a virtual key to unlock the device. So, a phisher may demand money from a victim. The phishers say they will give the key if the **ransom** is paid.

Some phishers target certain individuals to get information from a larger group. For example, victims may work for a company or government. These groups' computers are often connected. By hacking into one computer, phishers can steal much more company information. Then they can sell it online. Others can buy the information.

After natural disasters, people may be desperate. Phishers take advantage of that to trick people. Some phishers may pretend to be charities.

Phishing can also have political goals. For example, a group may oppose someone who is running for office. So, they spear phish people close to the candidate. Those victims' devices might hold important information about the candidate. Some information might make the candidate look bad. In that case,

In 2014, Sony Pictures got phished. The movie studio lost approximately $150 million.

phishers can publish the information. They may sell it to news organizations. The leak may hurt the candidate's chances.

Some governments use phishing during war. They target enemy governments or militaries. They may try to shut down **infrastructure**. Or they might try to gain access to key information. For example, a government might learn an enemy's battle plans.

Phishing attacks can be costly. Victims may have to pay workers to fix or fight the problems. Plus, phishing can make customers lose trust in a company. They may use other companies instead. So, the attacked company loses more money.

ATTACKING THE POWER GRID

In 2015, Russian hackers spear phished workers at Ukraine's power companies. They figured out which workers controlled the power grids. Then they hacked those workers' computers. Suddenly, about 225,000 people in Ukraine lost power. It was the first cyberattack to take out a power grid.

CHAPTER 4

FIGHTING PHISHING

People work to stop phishing in three major ways. Laws are one method. For example, identity theft is a crime. People who carry out phishing cyberattacks with that goal are breaking the law. Police officers catch those identity thieves. The phishers may have to pay fines. They may even go to prison.

Laws banning identity theft help prevent people from trying to phish.

In 2023, people reported about 300,000 phishing attempts to the FBI.

However, it is often hard to catch phishers. That's because hiding online crimes is sometimes easier than hiding other crimes. For example, other thieves may steal physical objects. They have to find the objects in person. Then they have to secretly get away. Police may already know what area those thieves are in. Police can also track who gets on planes.

In contrast, identity thieves can stay distant and hidden. They use **anonymous** accounts and sites. These accounts could be run by any of the billions of online users. After their crimes, phishers can disappear. They quickly delete those accounts or sites.

For these reasons, preventing phishing is important. That's why technology is another method of fighting phishing. Spam filters are a common anti-phishing technology. Filters look for patterns that are common in phishing. They might

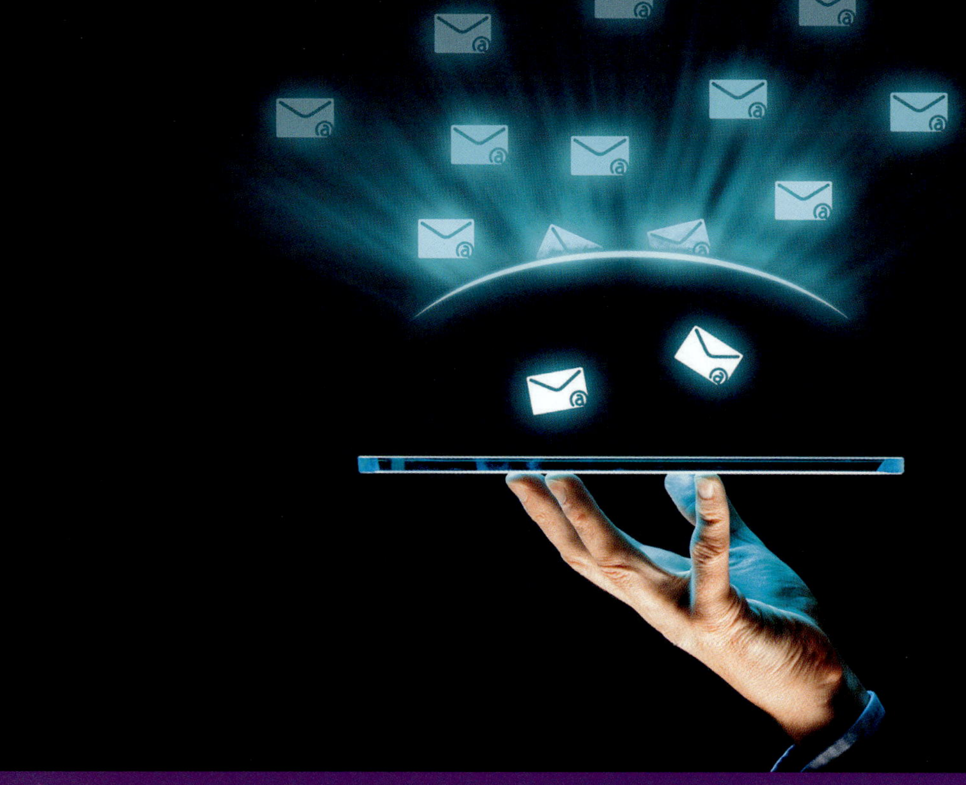

If spam filters work properly, only fake messages are blocked. Real ones still get through.

search for email addresses that have similar spellings to well-known ones. Then, the filters block messages from those addresses. That way, fewer people see phishing attempts.

However, technology has limits. For example, phishers can learn what spam filters look for. Then they come up with new methods. They may learn how to get past the filters.

Education is the third major way to fight phishing. Many companies and other groups hold regular meetings on the topic. They teach people the common signs of phishing. That way, people know what to look out for. They learn what information to keep safe. They can learn how to report possible phishing attempts, too.

Groups can offer education in several ways. For example, a company may carry out fake phishing attacks on its own workers. That way, the company can see

People are often the weakest part of a company's security. Training can help prevent problems.

how likely each person is to get tricked. Then the company can follow up. It can focus on helping people who need to learn the most about phishing.

Phishing methods are always changing. So, phishing education changes, too.

Many trainers might focus on phishing through email. But social media phishing is newer. People may not know as much about it. So, trainers create new programs to keep up.

GAMES AGAINST PHISHING

Some people learn best through games. So, people have created computer games about phishing. They teach players how to spot phishing. Players don't just listen to new information. They have to move through the game. They try to win by making the right choices. When players make a mistake, they can try again. They see what happens with a different choice. This approach can be fun. It also helps people remember what they've learned.

AVOIDING PHISHING

People can learn to avoid phishing attempts. There are some common signs to look out for. Phishing messages often use strong language. They play on big emotions, such as fear. They may offer solutions that seem too good to be true. Many phishing messages also ask for personal information.

Until people are sure a message is safe, they should not click any links or open any attachments. They should not enter their passwords or other information. Often, deleting the message is the best response.

Other security methods also help. For example, **two-factor authentication** is useful. It creates an extra step that can block phishers. Strong passwords are important. Using different

People should report phishing attempts as spam. That helps companies track phishing.

passwords for different accounts matters, too. That limits the harm if phishers get someone's password. The phishers can only get into one account.

FOCUS QUESTIONS

Write your answers on a separate piece of paper.

1. Write a paragraph explaining the main ideas of Chapter 3.
2. If you got a text that seemed like a phishing message, what would you do? Why?
3. What is one major way to help prevent phishing attacks?

    A. weak passwords
    B. phishing education
    C. ransomware

4. Why might phishers pretend to be credit card companies?

    A. so they can go to people's homes
    B. so they can learn people's account details
    C. so they can give away money

Answer key on page 32.

GLOSSARY

accounting
A job that involves keeping track of people's money.

anonymous
Involving someone whose name is kept secret or whose identity is not known.

artificial intelligence
The ability of a machine to make decisions on its own.

financial
Having to do with money.

hack
To illegally gain access to information on computer systems.

infrastructure
The systems, such as roads, water supplies, and energy distribution, that a place or company needs to function.

malware
Computer programs intended for a bad purpose.

ransom
Money paid to stop an attack.

two-factor authentication
Requiring two methods to access an account. It often involves a password and another device.

TO LEARN MORE

BOOKS

London, Martha. *Cybersecurity*. Bearport Publishing, 2023.

O'Sullivan, J. K. *Online Scams*. BrightPoint Press, 2022.

Thomas, Rachael L. *Digital Cryptology*. Lerner Publications, 2021.

NOTE TO EDUCATORS

Visit **www.focusreaders.com** to find lesson plans, activities, links, and other resources related to this title.

INDEX

Answer Key: 1. Answers will vary; 2. Answers will vary; 3. B; 4. B